to

....

....

A to Z

DEVOTIONS

FOR

BRAVE BOYS

MATT KOCEICH

BARBOUR kidz

A Division of Barbour Publishing

Cover and interior illustrations by Kevin Payne.

Published by Barbour Publishing, Inc., 1810 Barbour Drive, Uhrichsville, Ohio 44683, www.barbourbooks.com.

Our mission is to inspire the world with the life-changing message of the Bible.

Member of the
Evangelical Christian
Publishers Association

Printed in China.
002204 1024 XY

BRAVE BOYS ARE. . .

YOU ARE GOD'S BRAVE BOY!

What does it take to be a brave boy of God?

You'll find out in this fun devotional book created especially for you.

Each reading touches on a positive character trait—from A to Z:

Are you **A**dventurous? . . .

What about **G**enerous and **K**ind? . . .

Or **Loyal** and **W**ise? . . .

With each turn of the page, you'll be inspired to grow up God's way and become the brave boy He created you to be!

Brave Boys are
Adventurous!

Open your Bible and you will find tons of adventure stories. Noah took a wild ride on an ark with two of every kind of animal. Moses took a long journey to Egypt to have a conversation with the pharaoh. David traveled far from home to battle a person everyone else was too afraid to fight—the giant Goliath.

Just like each of these guys, you are special to God. He has big plans for your life.

One part of your lifetime adventure includes telling people about Jesus. God has given you power to go and share the Good News about what Jesus has done for all people. Your adventure starts with taking that first step!

THINK ABOUT IT:

Where do you think God is calling you to go first in your adventure of telling others about Jesus?

We thank God for the power Christ has given us.
He leads us and makes us win in everything.
He speaks through us wherever we go.
2 CORINTHIANS 2:14

Brave Boys are
BOLD!

Every single day of your life, God will help you to be bold. Being *bold* means that, as you live for God, you are confident and courageous. When God helps you to be brave and bold, you will start to see changes in your life. You won't worry about what other people think, because you'll be focused on who God says you are—His brave boy!

Nehemiah was bold when he helped rebuild a wall around Jerusalem so God's people would be protected. Nehemiah was bold because he knew who he was working for. . .God!

You can be bold, because you are God's brave boy!

THINK ABOUT IT:

When is it a good time for
you to be bold? At school? At home?

*[Paul] kept on preaching about the holy nation
of God. He taught about the Lord Jesus Christ
without fear. No one stopped him.*
ACTS 28:31

When you're on your way to becoming a brave boy, it's important to remember that God is always with you. And it's important to be considerate too.

What does it mean to be *considerate*? Considerate people think of others first. Jesus was a great example of a considerate person. He was always thinking about others. In fact, that's why He came to save us! It didn't matter if Jesus was around one person or a thousand people, He wanted to make sure everyone felt loved and cared for.

When you think about helping other people and think about their feelings too, you'll be making the most of your adventure with God!

THINK ABOUT IT:

How can you be considerate,
showing you care about others today?

■ ■ ■ ■ ■ ■ ■ ■ ■ ■ ■ ■ ■ ■ ■ ■ ■ ■ ■

Do not always be thinking about your own plans only.
Be happy to know what other people are doing.
PHILIPPIANS 2:4

Brave Boys are
DEPENDABLE!

Making good choices isn't always easy. Doing the right thing is hard sometimes, but remember that God is always there to help you, no matter what.

When someone is *dependable*, it means that person is trustworthy. There was a man named Joseph in the Bible who was very dependable. Joseph spent a long time in Egypt working for the pharaoh. His life wasn't always easy (he was even put in jail for something he didn't even do!), but Joseph put God first. People all around trusted Joseph because he was dependable, and he was eventually put in charge of a whole country!

Ask God to give you strength to make good choices. Being dependable is easier than you think!

THINK ABOUT IT:

What command in God's Word will you obey today?

- - - - - - - - - - - - - - -

But whoever obeys His Word has the love of God made perfect in him.
1 JOHN 2:5

Brave Boys are
EASYGOING!

Each person has a different type of personality, but as a brave boy, Jesus is calling you to be easygoing. He tells us in the Bible not to worry and not to be afraid. People who aren't easygoing stress and worry about everything.

Remember that God loves you always, and He has a great plan for your life. Let Him be in charge of everything you do. Knowing God is with you will help you grow into an easygoing boy who doesn't worry over every little thing.

Watch and see how being an easygoing, brave young boy will help you become a big blessing to others!

THINK ABOUT IT:

In what ways can you be more easygoing?

"Do not let your heart be troubled. You have put your trust in God, put your trust in Me also."
JOHN 14:1

F

Brave Boys are
FORGIVING!

Everybody makes mistakes sometimes. The cool thing about it is that if you ask God to forgive you, He does! In fact, His Word, the Bible, says that we should be quick to forgive others too.

Forgiveness is much easier when you're connected to God. Make sure you spend time reading your Bible every day. That's one way you can be sure you're connected with Him. God's Word will also help you to remember that forgiving someone can help show them who Jesus is too. Then the next step to becoming a brave boy is to forgive someone who has hurt you. . .it's true. With God's help, you can do it!

THINK ABOUT IT:

Who do you need to forgive today?

Forgive other people just as God forgave you because of Christ's death on the cross.
EPHESIANS 4:32

Brave Boys are
GENEROUS!

The Bible is full of stories of generous people. If someone is *generous*, that means he or she gives *more* than what's expected.

Time is a gift that is important to everyone, but it's a gift that is often very hard to give away because the world is such a busy place. If you give time to your mom, that might mean you help her around the house. That's one example of generosity.

The apostle Paul gave all his time to tell the world about Jesus. King David spent a great deal of time writing the psalms so people would know how great God is. Being generous is a very good way to grow as a brave boy of God.

THINK ABOUT IT:

Come up with a plan to show generosity
to a family member or friend.

■ ■ ■ ■ ■ ■ ■ ■ ■ ■ ■ ■ ■ ■ ■ ■ ■

We must remember what the Lord Jesus said,
"We are more happy when we give than when we receive."
ACTS 20:35

Brave Boys are HONEST!

Being honest—always telling the truth—is a great way to live each day. It builds good character; and you want to be known as someone who can be counted on, don't you? Part of God's plan is to use you, His brave boy, as a blessing to others.

Did you know that being honest helps you grow closer to God? In fact, when you are honest, you bring God glory.

There was a man in the Bible named Peter. He was a close friend of Jesus. One time, Peter lied to get out of trouble, but it didn't make him feel good. . .and he realized he should always tell the truth.

Today, ask Jesus to give you the courage to always be honest.

THINK ABOUT IT:

When is it hard to tell the truth?
Why is it important to always be honest?

Do not lie to each other. You have put out of your life your old ways.
COLOSSIANS 3:9

Brave Boys are
IMAGINATIVE!

God is so creative. Just look at the world around you! The big blue sky. Fluffy clouds. Beautiful songbirds. Large shade trees. Animals of all shapes and sizes. People—no two alike! Everything is so unique in its own way. And you. . .when God made you, He gave you many special gifts and talents. Your imagination and the ability to create things are such awesome gifts!

There are so many ways to put your imagination to use. You can write a story or paint a picture. You can design a house or plant a garden. Using your mind to think about helping other people is a great quality too. Think about creative ways to be a good friend, and just watch and see how that helps bring a smile to someone else today.

THINK ABOUT IT:

How can you use your creativity
to tell someone about Jesus?

*In the beginning God made from nothing
the heavens and the earth.*

GENESIS 1:1

Brave Boys are
JOYFUL!

The word *joyful* means being really, really happy. Is there something that really makes you super happy? Maybe it's playing with your friends or watching a funny movie. Or maybe reading a funny book that makes you laugh.

Sometimes things happen and you may not always feel happy. That's okay, because the Bible tells us that God loves His children and can give them happy hearts. This happens when we pray and read the Bible. When we do these things, we are trusting that God will take care of us. And knowing that God cares for you is something you can always be really happy about!

THINK ABOUT IT:

How can you work on being
joyful in all areas of your life?

■-■-■-■-■-■-■-■-■-■-■-■-■-■-■

*Our hope comes from God. May He fill you with joy
and peace because of your trust in Him.*
Romans 15:13

Brave Boys are
KIND!

Doesn't it make you feel good when people are nice? Becoming a brave boy doesn't happen by chance. It's a choice. Kindness includes choosing to treat everyone in a friendly way. Maybe you can be kind with your words. Maybe you can be a good listener to a friend who needs someone to talk to.

There's a Bible story about a man who helped someone who was hurt. Several people walked by the person who needed help and completely ignored him. But then this man—the Good Samaritan—was the first and only person to show kindness. He made sure the man's needs were met and even left money to take care of his future needs. That's true kindness!

THINK ABOUT IT:

What are some ways you can show kindness to others?

Because of this, we should do good to everyone.
GALATIANS 6:10

Brave Boys are LOYAL!

Do you know what *loyalty* means? It means showing your support for someone or something. When you are loyal, you work hard at whatever you do. A brave boy who is loyal works hard for his teachers. He is known for treating everyone with respect. He lives out each day knowing that whatever he does for others, he is doing the same for Jesus.

There was a lady named Esther in the Old Testament who was very loyal. She risked her life to make sure her people were protected. She honored God with the decisions she made, because she knew that doing the right thing was very important!

THINK ABOUT IT:

Who can you show loyalty and
support to by your actions?

----

*Whatever work you do, do it with all your heart.
Do it for the Lord and not for men.*
COLOSSIANS 3:23

Brave Boys are
MANNERLY!

Being polite. Treating others the way you want to be treated. That's what being mannerly is all about. Brave boys like you set a great example by making good choices. The adults in your life, as well as your friends, watch how you act. A mannerly, brave boy isn't rude or selfish, but he thinks of others and finds ways to be respectful.

Caring about what other people are going through and trying to be a good friend is another way to show manners. Saying "Yes, Sir," and "Yes, Ma'am" are good ways to be mannerly too. Showing good manners communicates to people that you are a boy who is courageous!

THINK ABOUT IT:

Is it hard to always be mannerly? Why or why not?

If we live in the light as He is in the light, we share what we have in God with each other. And the blood of Jesus Christ, His Son, makes our lives clean from all sin.
1 JOHN 1:7

Brave Boys are
NOBLE!

When you think of someone who's noble, maybe you think of a king or queen, or even a knight who is brave enough to devote his life to protect the royal family. Picture a noble soldier on horseback, with his shield and sword standing up for truth.

As a brave boy living life for God, you are someone with big ideas who cares about doing the right thing. You are noble like the knight. You think about setting an example and helping your family any way you can. You always want what's best and choose to do the right thing. Being noble is a good way to respect yourself and others!

THINK ABOUT IT:

In what ways can you be noble and serve others?

But the man of honor makes good plans,
and he stands for what is good.
ISAIAH 32:8

Brave Boys are
OBEDIENT!

B rave boys do everything like they're doing it for Jesus! If Jesus asked you to do something, you'd do it, right? Brave boys like you obey their parents and teachers. They set a good example for their friends by doing what they're told.

Jesus was obedient when He willingly died on the cross for our sins. He said that He wanted His Father's will to be done. Think about it like this: when you obey, you are being like Jesus. Isn't that something really wonderful?

Practice being brave and follow directions the first time someone asks you to do something. When you obey, you are shining your light bright for Jesus.

THINK ABOUT IT:

How does obeying make you more like Jesus?

"Love the Lord your God. Always do what He tells you and keep all His Laws."
DEUTERONOMY 11:1

Brave Boys are
PATIENT!

It's so hard to wait. Our world is all about speed. Microwaves help us cook our meals quickly. Smartphones help us research information and get answers within seconds; they also help us connect with people superfast.

Jesus showed us a great picture of what patience looks like when He fed five thousand people. The crowd was hungry, and Jesus and His friends had had a busy day. They were tired. It would have been easy for Jesus to ignore the crowd and let them go find food on their own. But Jesus knew that being patient with them was important. So He did a miracle and fed all of the people (with only five loaves of bread and two fish!) and even waited for all of them to finish eating.

Be brave. Patiently wait for God. He will *always* come through for you!

THINK ABOUT IT:

What is one thing that you are waiting on?
Can you make a decision to be patient?

■-■-■-■-■-■-■-■-■-■-■-■-■-■-■

*Wait for the Lord. Be strong. Let your heart
be strong. Yes, wait for the Lord.*
PSALM 27:14

Brave Boys are
QUIET!

Do you know what it means to be quiet before the Lord? Brave boys practice being quiet when they spend time alone reading God's Word. The Bible says that we should "be still" and know that He is God.

The world is a busy place. People go to work and school. They go to the store and to doctor's appointments. Maybe they have sports practice. There are a ton of things in life that demand your attention. And then there's TV and video games too.

Brave boys work on tuning out all the world's noise so they can focus on God. Find ways throughout your day to "be still" and focus on God, who is leading you to do great things!

THINK ABOUT IT:

When can you make time each day
to be quiet and read your Bible?

- - - - - - - - - - - - - - - -

"The Lord will fight for you.
All you have to do is keep still."
EXODUS 14:14

Brave Boys are
RESPONSIBLE!

Responsible boys find ways to help others. They ask their teachers for ways they can help in the classroom. When they are in the school cafeteria or at home, they clean up after themselves. This blesses the custodians and parents. Brave boys who practice being responsible don't wait for a parent to tell them what to do. Instead, they do what's expected of them, and they can be counted on to do the right thing (even without being asked!).

Bravery looks like a soldier who is prepared for battle. And even though you are young, you can show your friends and the adults in your life that you are prepared for the responsibilities you've been given. God is very proud of you!

THINK ABOUT IT:

What is one chore you can focus on doing without being reminded to do it?

"He that is faithful with little things is faithful with big things also."
LUKE 16:10

Brave Boys are
STRONG!

Brave and *strong* are great words to describe you as you keep living your life for Jesus. Strength doesn't just come from lifting weights at the gym. Strength also means sticking up for what's right.

With God's help, you can do great things because He gives you strength. You might have a friend who does something wrong, like laugh at someone because they're different. Being brave and strong will help you do the right thing and not laugh.

When you practice being strong, you will stand out in the crowd. Instead of following others, you will be a strong leader who loves to obey God's Word.

THINK ABOUT IT:

When have you shown strength by sticking up for what's right? How did it make you feel?

For God did not give us a spirit of fear. He gave us a spirit of power and of love and of a good mind.
2 TIMOTHY 1:7

Brave Boys are
THANKFUL!

The Bible teaches us to always be thankful. A good way to practice this is by keeping a notebook and making a list of all the things that you're thankful for. Keeping your focus on how God blesses you will help you stay positive.

There was a lady who was sad because she didn't have any friends. Jesus met her at a well and reminded her that she mattered to God. The woman was so happy that she ran home and told her whole village about Jesus. Because of her thankful heart, many people in the town believed in Jesus!

Be thankful and watch how people around you will start asking why you're so happy. Then you can tell them all about Jesus!

THINK ABOUT IT:

What do you have to be thankful for?
Make a list today!

Always give thanks for all things to God the Father
in the name of our Lord Jesus Christ.
EPHESIANS 5:20

Brave Boys are
UNSELFISH!

It's hard to think about other people's feelings and what they're going through. When you have so much to do every day, it's easy to become selfish. Being *unselfish* means just the opposite—it's choosing to act like Jesus acted. Doing things for others or giving up something you really want is the way you practice real unselfishness.

Jesus was unselfish all the time. He made sure people had what they needed. One time, when He was praying, Jesus was sad because it was almost time for Him to die for our sins on the cross. Even though Jesus was about to go through a very hard time, He prayed for all believers! He wants you to be encouraged by His love and live unselfishly.

THINK ABOUT IT:

Who can you pray for today? If you see that person, be unselfish and do or say something nice to make their day special.

"You are to love each other. You must love each other as I have loved you."
JOHN 13:34

*V*aliant means having a lot of courage. It also means you are determined to do what you know is right.

A man named Joshua loved God very much. He was a scout in charge of finding land for God's people. Some of the other scouts were afraid, but not Joshua—he had faith. He listened as God told him to be valiant.

If you know the story, you'll remember that Joshua was one of the courageous and determined soldiers who marched around the big, walled city of Jericho. Joshua watched the walls fall down, just as God said they would.

As you grow every day into the brave boy God created you to be, think about how you can be valiant!

THINK ABOUT IT:

Who are some valiant people you know?
What makes them valiant?

"Be strong and have strength of heart! Do not be afraid or lose faith. For the Lord your God is with you anywhere you go."
JOSHUA 1:9

Brave Boys are
WISE!

Wisdom comes from learning God's truth—God's truth is everything that's in your Bible. When you know what God thinks is important, it will be easier to make good decisions. When you know what God says is right, it will help guide your steps.

There was a brave young man named Daniel who always prayed. He was very wise, because doing what God wanted was the most important thing to him. There were people who tried getting Daniel in trouble, but God protected him.

Spend time reading Bible stories and see how people who obeyed God were blessed. Be wise and thankful for all the ways God takes care of you!

THINK ABOUT IT:

Which one of God's lessons can
you apply to your life today?

■ ■ ■ ■ ■ ■ ■ ■ ■ ■ ■ ■ ■ ■ ■ ■

But the wisdom that comes from heaven is first of all pure.
Then it gives peace. It is gentle and willing to obey.
JAMES 3:17

Brave Boys are
e**X**TRAORDINARY!

A brave boy's life is a very special life. It's a life that shows the world who Jesus is and what He's like. It's an extraordinary life, because it makes a big deal of God.

An ordinary life goes through the motions, but extraordinary living does much more. It serves other people by letting them know they matter to God. It is unselfish and loving, just like Jesus.

Maybe it's giving your teacher a compliment. Maybe it's doing your chores at home without being asked. Maybe being extraordinary is holding the door open for your mom. It's that easy. Get good at finding ways to be a blessing to others. Then people will see Jesus in your extraordinary living.

THINK ABOUT IT:

What extraordinary things can you do to show others how wonderful God is?

When you heard the truth, you put your trust in Christ. Then God marked you by giving you His Holy Spirit as a promise.
EPHESIANS 1:13

Brave Boys are
YOUNG!

You are young because of your physical age, but brave boys also think about how they can have a young attitude in everything they do. An old and tired attitude says, "No, I'm going to do things my way. I don't like change." But young attitudes are full of energy and willingness to do a job for God.

This is what happened when the disciples were fishing all night and didn't catch anything. Jesus told them to go back out and try again. The disciples took Jesus seriously and found strength to take the boat to deeper water. They caught so much fish after listening to Jesus that their nets ripped!

Be brave and always keep a young attitude when it comes to working. God is proud of you!

THINK ABOUT IT:

How can you build up energy to have a "young" attitude and serve well?

How can a young man keep his way pure? By living by Your Word.
PSALM 119:9

Brave Boys are
ZEALOUS!

Being *zealous* is when you get really, *really* excited about something. Fans of sports teams are zealous in the way they cheer for their favorite teams.

Brave boys are also zealous when they live their lives for God. They act like Paul in the New Testament, who went on four huge missionary trips to preach the Gospel. Paul was so excited to share Jesus with anyone who would listen. He didn't worry about himself. He just was zealous for God, even though he had many hardships along the way.

Jesus was excited too. He spent His whole life doing God's will. How about you? Where will your excitement for God lead you?

THINK ABOUT IT:

How can you show your excitement for God?

- -

I can do all things because
Christ gives me the strength.
PHILIPPIANS 4:13

MORE ENCOURAGEMENT AND WISDOM FOR BRAVE BOYS LIKE YOU!

100 Adventurous Stories for Brave Boys

Boys are history-makers! And this deeply compelling storybook proves it! This collection of 100 adventurous stories of Christian men—from the Bible, history, and today—will empower you to know and understand how men of great character have made an impact in the world and how much smaller our faith (and the biblical record) would be without them.

Paperback / 978-1-63609-999-6